PRIVATE

PRIVATE

PHOTOGRAPHS BY ALISON JACKSON

FOREWORD

Celebrities surround us. They're everywhere we go. In the papers, online and in our social media feeds. They become such a familiar part of our everyday lives that we feel as if we know them. When, in fact, we only really know them through their photographic images.

I first explored this phenomenon after the death of Diana. We felt we knew her intimately yet very few people had actually met her for real. When she died, the world mourned. But we did not mourn the woman so much as her iconic image – the one presented to us by the media.

Today, our fascination continues, whether it's the Duke and Duchess of Cambridge, or this generation's King and Queen of Celebrity: 'Kimye'.

In my work I use cleverly crafted actors and celebrity lookalikes to create images that pose fundamental questions about where the truth ends and lies begin. The line between what is real and what is fantasy has never been more blurred. My photographs seek to explore the gap between the two and, if only for a second, bring it sharply into focus.

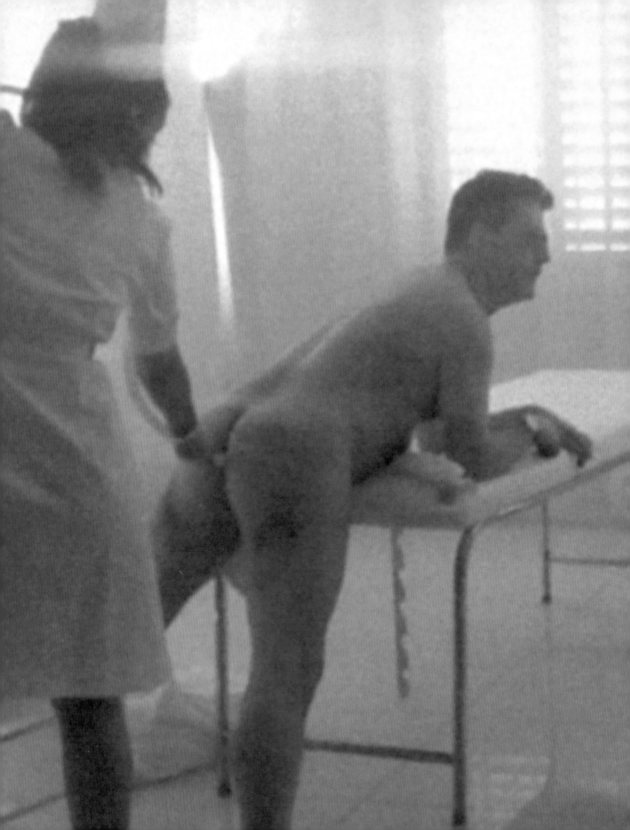

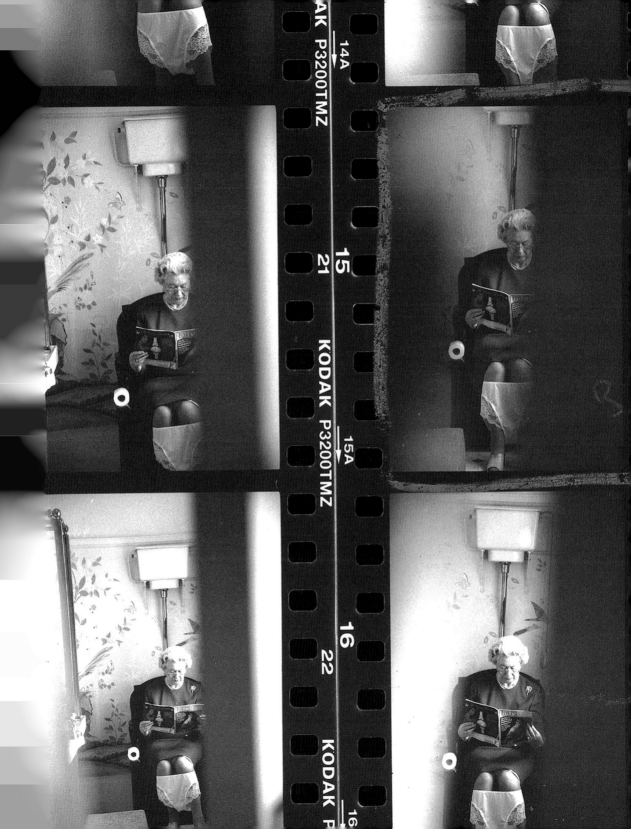

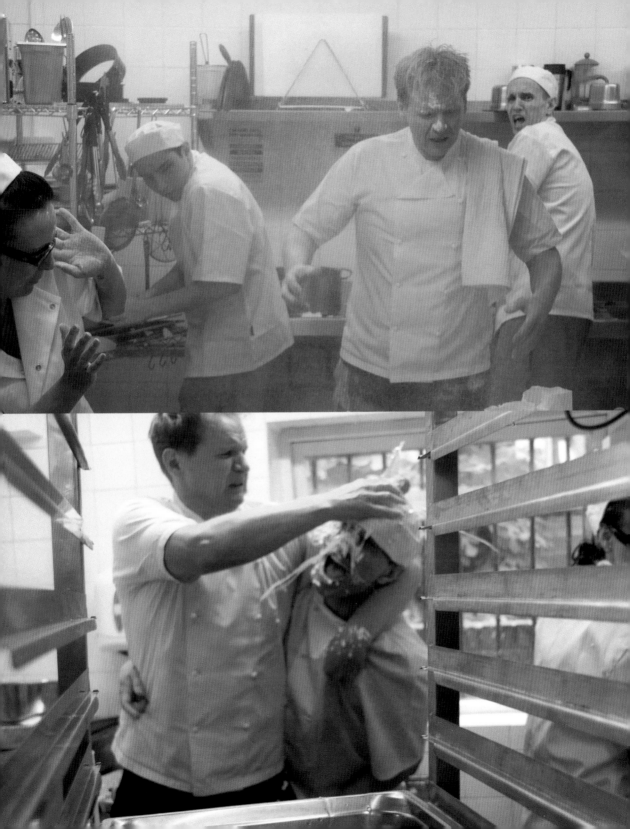

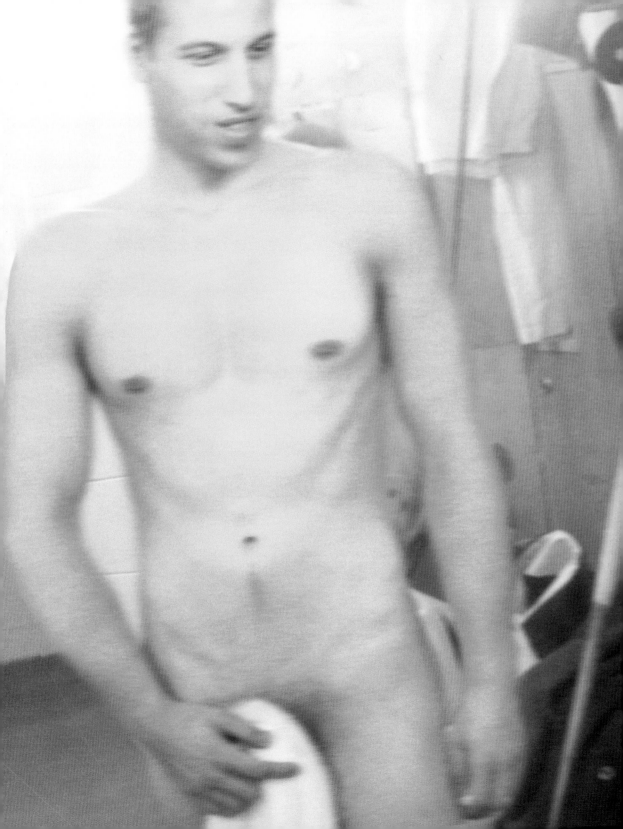

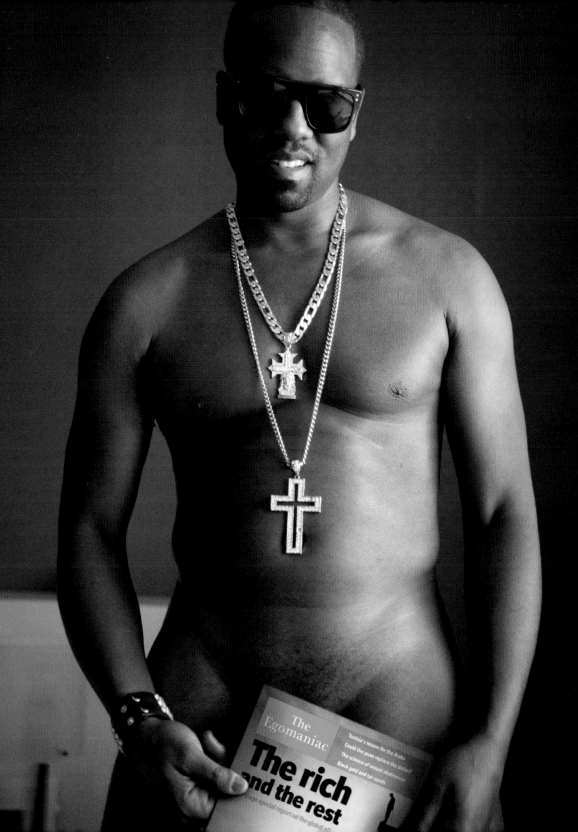

The Egomaniac

Tunisia's lesson for the Arabs
Could the yuan replace the dollar?
The science of sexual abstinence
Black gold and tar sands

The rich
and the rest

A 14-page special report on the global elite

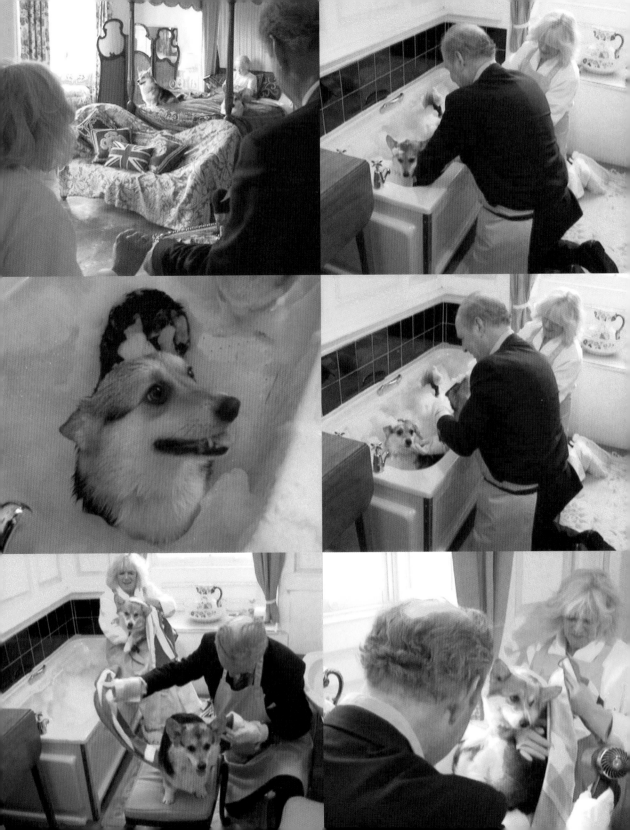

PUBLISHER

Alison Jackson Publishing Ltd.
134 Lots Road, London SW10 0RJ, United Kingdom

Printed in Macedonia by Branko Gapo Printing Ltd
Edition 02
ISBN: 978-1-911556-01-5

ACKNOWLEDGEMENTS

I thank everyone who was involved in the making of these photographs and book.

Special thanks to Tom Rawstorne and Denny Einav who helped write the scenes.

I thank all my crew who have painstakingly crafted each photograph in detail to replicate the real deal as much as possible. The high-quality production is a result of their hard work including scouting locations and set building; sourcing and making costumes; meticulous styling of wigs and hair; lighting and photography; and detailed editing and retouching from technicians who are also artists.

Elizabeth Carmody (Producer), Natasha Cheek (Art Department), Andrew Farrer and Andrew Bailey (Photography), Per Krogh (Video), Michele Cadei (DOP), Amy Wilson, Henrik Torp, Terri Pace and An Pham (Hair and Makeup), Julien Bader McConnell, Karin Gunnarsson and Leo LeBeau (Retouching), Tapestry (Post-Production), Dani Matthews Studio (Book Design).

I thank all the people and companies that have commissioned me and allowed me to make my own work: Vanity Fair, Condé Nast, Cosmopolitan, Fox, BBC, Sky, Mr. President, DDB, The Body Shop, Not on the High Street, Microsoft, Kleenex and Costa – to name just a few.

A big thank you to Philip DeBevoise, Tim Hughes and Francesca Barra.

Special thanks also to Stefano Pasianot and Toyin Gbadamosi.

I am indebted to all the actors and lookalikes who have transformed what we imagine into a photographic reality.

I am an ambassador for The Spinal Injuries Association: www.spinal.co.uk. A portion of profits from this book will be donated to the charity.

ALISON JACKSON is a BAFTA and multi-award winning contemporary artist who explores the cult of celebrity – an extraordinary phenomenon created by the media and publicity industries. Jackson makes convincingly realistic work about celebrities doing things in private using lookalikes. Likeness becomes real and fantasy touches on the believable.

Her work has established wide respect for her as an incisive, funny and thought-provoking commentator on the burgeoning spectacle of contemporary celebrity culture. She works across all media and arts platforms including TV, books …and even opera.

Jackson has exhibited in galleries and museums worldwide including Tate Modern, London, Centre Pompidou in Paris and the San Francisco Museum of Modern Art (SFMOMA). She has been invited to numerous panel discussions and has given a TED Talk on her work.

Alison Jackson lives in London but will go to the ends of the earth to find just the right lookalike.

Twitter @alisonjackson
Instagram @alisonjackson
www.alisonjackson.com

My aim is to explore the blurred boundaries between reality and the imaginary – the gap and confusion between the two. I use lookalikes of celebrities and public figures to create a seemingly real documentary scenario which is in fact a fiction. Likeness becomes real and fantasy touches on the believable. The viewer is suspended in disbelief. I try to highlight the psychological relationship between what we see and what we imagine. This is bound up in our need to look – our voyeurism – and our need to believe.

My work is about simulation. Creating a clone or a copy of the 'real' on paper. It is not a fake, it takes the place of the 'real' for a moment. As Baudrillard puts it, simulation is different from feigning. Feigning is pretending, such as, feigning illness or pretending to be ill. The subject is not ill, just seeming to be, but 'simulation threatens the difference between 'true' and 'false', between 'real' and 'imaginary'. Since the simulator produces 'true' symptoms - is he ill or not? He cannot be treated objectively either as 'ill' or 'not ill'.'

This is what I aim to do: create likeness of icons, where in image – on paper – the simulation of icons 'threatens the difference between 'true' and 'false', between 'real' and 'imaginary'.' The real subject becomes 'not necessary'. The image or icon is more important and more seductive. It doesn't matter if it isn't the 'real' icon – as long as it looks like him or her – it creates a temporary confusion. I search for this confusion and aim to create it within my work.

I explore to what extent I should create complete fantasy pictures not connected to anything 'true' or 'real' and the relevance of the connection of something 'true'. I believe that you cannot rely on your own perception when it comes to photography. I prove the camera lies.

Baudrillard, Jean, 'The Procession of Simulacra' in Brian Wallis, (ed.), *Art after Modernism; Rethinking Representation,* Boston: Godline, 1984 (253-81).

EXHIBITIONS OF ALISON JACKSON'S WORKS

2017: Haifa Musuem of Art, 2016: Villa Rot, Germany; 2015: NRW Forum, Düsseldorf; 2014: Centre Pompidou, Paparazzi Paris; 2014: Schirn Museum, Paparazzi, Frankfurt; 2012: Paris Photo, Le Louvre, Paris; 2011: Ben Brown Fine Art London; 2011: The Hayward Gallery, The Royal Family, London; 2011: SFMOMA: Exposed, San Francisco; 201 KunstHalle Amsterdam, Peeping Tom; 2010: Tate Modern, Voyeurism, London; 2010: Tate Britain, Rude Britannia London; 2008: Hamiltons Gallery, London; 2008: Liverpool Biennial International Festival of Contemporary Art, New A Gallery, UK; 2008: Musée de L'Eysée, Lausanne; 2007: Institute of Contemporary Arts (ICA), London, New York; 200 KunstForum, Vienna; 2004: Hayward Gallery, London; 2003: Le Mois de la Photo, Montreal; 2003: International Center of Photography (ICP), New York.

AWARDS

BAFTA, Infinity Award, D&AD, Photographers Gallery and Best of the Best, amongst others.